# embellish
## *and* stitch

VALERIE CAMPBELL-HARDING and MAGGIE GREY

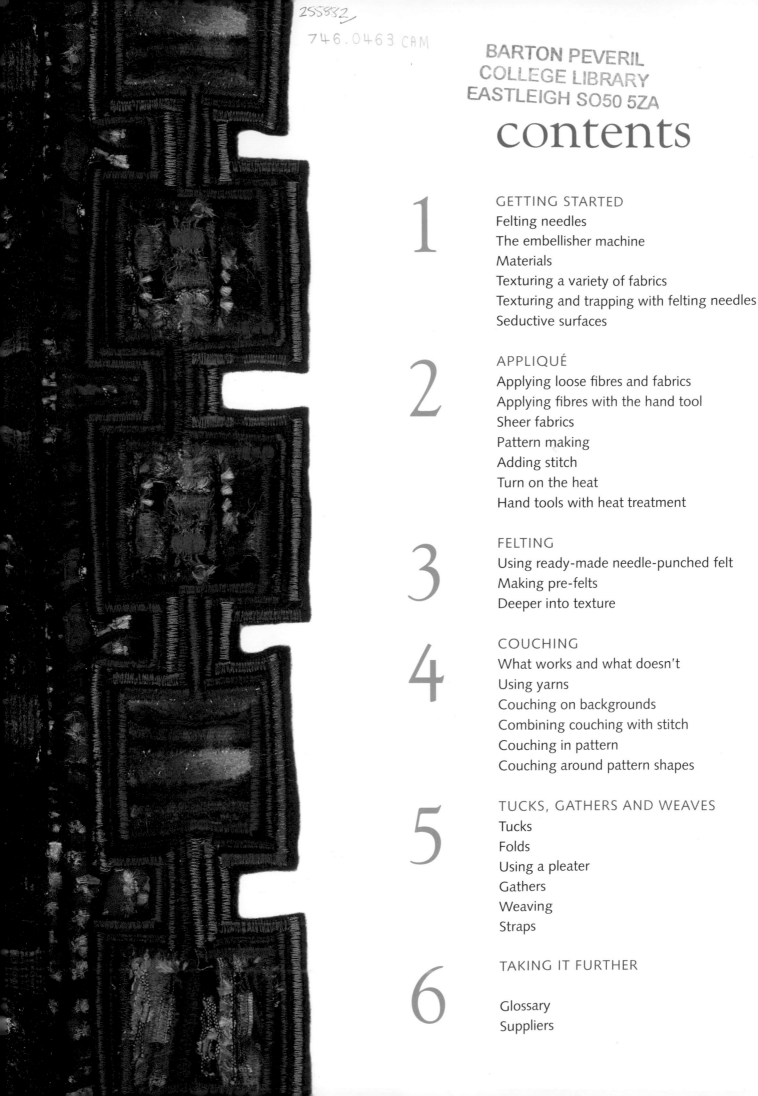

# contents

**1**  GETTING STARTED     6
Felting needles
The embellisher machine
Materials
Texturing a variety of fabrics
Texturing and trapping with felting needles
Seductive surfaces

**2**  APPLIQUÉ     16
Applying loose fibres and fabrics
Applying fibres with the hand tool
Sheer fabrics
Pattern making
Adding stitch
Turn on the heat
Hand tools with heat treatment

**3**  FELTING     30
Using ready-made needle-punched felt
Making pre-felts
Deeper into texture

**4**  COUCHING     36
What works and what doesn't
Using yarns
Couching on backgrounds
Combining couching with stitch
Couching in pattern
Couching around pattern shapes

**5**  TUCKS, GATHERS AND WEAVES     44
Tucks
Folds
Using a pleater
Gathers
Weaving
Straps

**6**  TAKING IT FURTHER     52

Glossary
Suppliers

A strap made by embellishing stitched leaves, cut
pieces of previously embellished fabric and shreds
of metallic organza onto net.

# introduction

Felting needles and commercial needle-felting machines have been around for a long time. Felt made with hand-held felting needles has been enjoying something of a come-back, especially for three-dimensional work. Recently, the domestic version of the machine has been taken up by textile artists. Generally known as an embellishing machine, it looks like a sewing machine but that is where the resemblance ends: no top thread, no bobbin, just a circle of sharp, barbed needles that mesh fabrics together. It can be used for a variety of applications such as making new fabrics, enhancing and adding texture to existing ones, and combining with machine and hand stitching. For all these uses and more, it is a valuable addition to the embroiderer's workroom.

Often described as a dry felting machine, the embellisher certainly short-circuits the felting process. It produces needle-punched felts that can be water- and heat-treated to make full felts or can be left at the partially-felted stage for further embellishment. However, the machine can be used for much more than just felting and this book covers a wide range of applications, from simple texturing of sheer fabrics (which can produce amazing effects) to building up more complex designs with stitch. The fact that there is no thread colour to intervene between maker and machine is very liberating, especially where colour planning is involved, and the speed of working adds an unexpected dynamism. We give practical advice and tips on using and maintaining the machine, choosing materials and combining with stitch.

This book is not just for those who own an embellisher. It also offers ideas for using felting needles and working by hand – and not just for felting. You'll be surprised what can be achieved with unusual fabrics, fibres and adventurous techniques.

By hand or machine, you'll find a range of exciting options being explored throughout, with ideas for finished pieces using the techniques.

RIGHT: Vessel made by embellishing wool tops onto pelmet Vilene.
*(Carolyn Sinclair)*

# felting needles

You can buy these singly or in groups, set into handles. They all have barbs on the needle shaft for meshing the layers of fabric together. The most common needles have triangular blades with the barb close to the tip of the needle. Star blades are more robust but are not always easy to find. Needles come in a range of sizes (gauges) with the higher gauge being finer. For heavy work, use a 19 gauge; 40 for very fine work.

Different techniques call for a variety of needles. The ones set into a handle are excellent for texturing fabrics – as you can see in the piece below. Single needles are great for use with pre-felts and especially so in three-dimensional work. You will also need a foam pad to work on; the best ones are those made as kneeling pads for gardeners. The needles cannot be used in exactly the same way as the embellisher machine but there are lots of suggestions in the relevant chapters for achieving similar results.

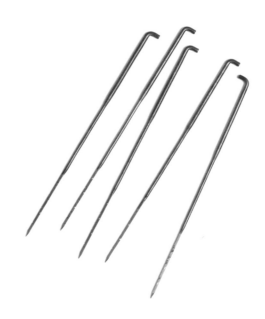

# the embellisher machine

The machine itself requires very little maintenance apart from cleaning. The needles do break and they are expensive to replace but breakage can be minimised by following a few simple suggestions.

- Guide the fabric gently, don't tug.
- Make sure that the screw which controls the foot height is as low as it will go. It is tempting to leave it set high so you don't have to lift it to remove the fabric but this is a certain way to break needles. This screw may be on the top of the machine or on the back of the needle assembly.
- Remember to lift the needles and the foot when removing work. It is all too easy to leave the foot down and this may cause the needles to catch.
- Don't try to stitch on fabrics that are too hard. The embellisher likes soft fabrics and will break needles if used on hard fabrics or heavy paper. Avoid slubs and string. Soft is best; listen to the machine and don't let it struggle.
- When using loose fibres or fine chiffon, try to keep them flat to the fabric or pat them down well. Otherwise they may get caught in the needle guard which will entail a certain amount of clipping away. If you get a big jam then cut the fabric free, remove the needle assembly and clear it. Better still, lay some coarse net over the top and pull it away when you have finished. It won't stick.

ABOVE and RIGHT: The embellisher machine was designed for making needle-punched felt. However, there are more interesting uses for these machines and they include texturing fabrics, appliqué and couching.

The running of the machine over the fabric is referred to in this book as *needling* or *embellishing*.

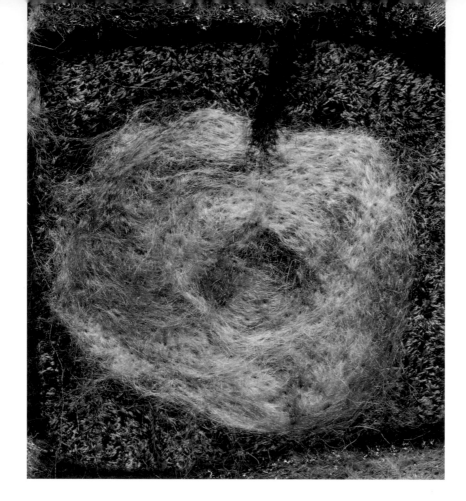

A machine embroidered apple with wool fibres applied using the embellisher.

Try not to have very thick layers; we don't always follow this suggestion and sometimes resign ourselves to losing needles. A good test is to try it with the hand wheel first. If you have problems pushing the needles through by hand then it really is too thick or tough.

Your instruction book will tell you how to change needles. When the machine is new, the tiny screws are often hard to undo and, for the first change, it may be worth using a stronger Allen key than the one provided. When you have changed the needle and replaced the housing, make sure that the needles are central to the holes in the plate before the final tightening of the screw, and adjust if they are not. If they are a little one-sided, they can bend.

# materials

Soft fabrics are the safest to use. Firmer fabrics can be applied and we'll look at them later. The best way to start is to lay in supplies of fibres such as nylon, wool or silk tops, as they'll be used a lot throughout this book and can be applied, layered or blended in many ways. Ordinary commercial felt makes a good backing fabric and can be purchased by the metre from most fabric shops. Fine chiffon is invaluable – see below.

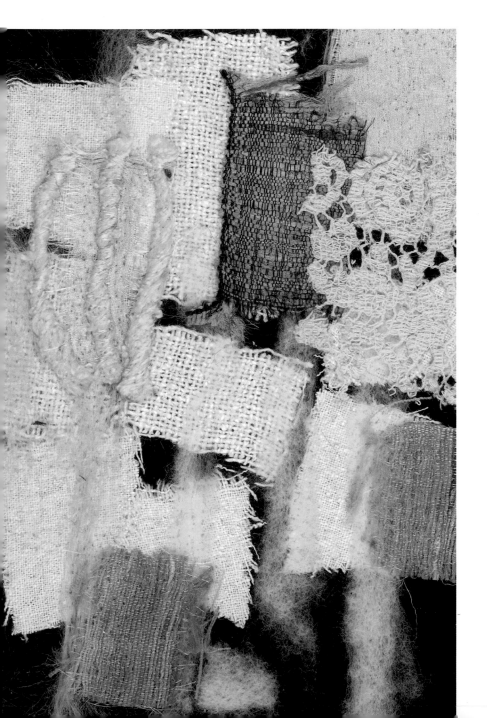

Here are some other fabrics to look out for.

- Sheer fabrics such as organza will also be useful and cheap commercial felt is a very good ground fabric. Fine chiffon scarves can be wonderful, especially when the heat tool is used.
- Silk fabrics are magic when embellished (apart from very stiff or slubby ones). Small torn pieces of coloured silk merge into backgrounds beautifully and the edges can be blended easily so that they disappear.
- Scrim, soft bandaging and other such materials will also have a place in the fabric stash.
- Yarns can be applied, so look out for some unusual ones: textured, hairy, fuzzy, glitzy, all are useful. The recent upsurge in knitting has brought a wealth of goodies to even the smallest wool shop.

Samples of silk fabrics embellished on black felt. Silks embellish beautifully and the edges blend perfectly with the background.

Keep an eye out in charity shops for patterned scarves in lightweight materials. These embellish beautifully – the more colourful the better, as the colour will be knocked back by varying the background fabric. It is, of course, possible to paint your own material and a fine silk, painted with silk paints, will also perform well.

Try to find unusual fabrics in such places as furniture stores. I found the wonderful voile below with the net curtains. The lettering looks great when embellished by hand or machine. Other patterned fabrics, those of a heavier composition, shouldn't be discounted provided they are not too stiff. They often give exciting results on the reverse as a broken pattern emerges.

ABOVE: Sheer non-woven fabric with interesting lettering, found in the curtain department of a store, was needled onto commercial felt which had already been embellished with wool fibres. A piece of computer-printed tissue was then applied. The next stage of this work can be seen on page 45.

BELOW: Look in the curtain department of a store for interesting fabrics such as this one.

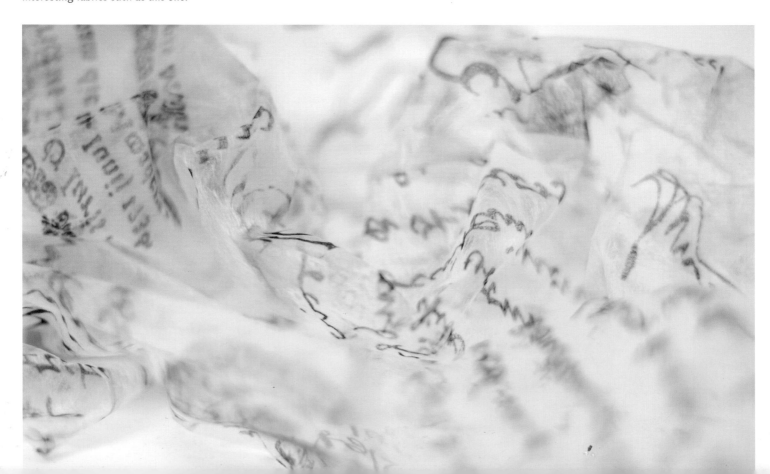

# texturing a variety of fabrics

Sheer fabrics such as organza or fine silk can be used to create an amazing textured surface when used alone with the embellisher. They should not be too 'floppy'. Fine chiffon, for instance, could just disappear into the needle hole if not held firmly. Run something like a crystal organza under the machine and look at the result. Now try taking a wide strip of the same fabric and running the embellisher (needling) down the centre. Note how it pleats the fabric.

Having explored a variety of fabrics, try some of the following.

- Leave some areas untextured, either in random bursts or in a pattern.
- Trap some yarn, fabric scraps or snippets of thread between layers of sheer fabric and work over them.
- Lay the sheer fabric on a background and work in a pattern which could be enhanced with lines of free machining.
- Try using a soft silk and working into it to give textured areas.

BELOW: Silk fabrics and tops embellished onto a woven silk fabric.

BELOW: Fine silk habotai embellished to make a pattern, leaving empty spaces.

# texturing and trapping with felting needles

For this exercise, use two sheer fabrics. In the examples below I used a synthetic organza and a black chiffon scarf. Use one of the felting tools with as many needles as possible. The one shown has four needles. Work as follows.

- Lay the fabrics on top of each other on a hard surface like a chopping board. Be very aware that the needles are sharp and mind your fingers. Start by placing the tool in the middle of the fabrics and pulling them up around it.
- Keep working like this until the fabrics are joined together all over. You'll note how they have ruched and that the fabrics are distressed. Now try turning the tool upside down and pulling the fabrics down over it. **Mind your fingers.**
- When you have achieved a good surface texture, lay some silk, nylon or wool fibres on top and place the needles over it. Pull up the fabrics as before.

Try this technique using different fabrics, perhaps a habotai silk. Trapping yarns or snippets of fabric in the middle of two sheers also works well. Just sandwich them between the fabrics and work as described.

This fabric can be placed over a base of felt and stitched by hand, with added beads. It can also be free machined or could form a base for some of the appliqué techniques shown later in the book.

Two pieces of sheer fabric have been distressed with a hand felting needle. A little glitzy nylon was added. This piece will be machine stitched to commercial felt.

# seductive surfaces

The embellishing machine can be used to build surface textures which will stand alone or form the background for further embroidery. There are many ways to achieve these effects, depending on the materials and techniques used.

Cheap commercial felt is one of the best fabrics to use as a base for layering up further materials. If the felt is to be covered completely and worked into, any colour can be used. However, if it is going to be part of the work, consideration should be given to the colour. Black is often a dramatic colour, especially when used with bright wool tops or silks. Felt takes up a lot of paint but it could be dyed, perhaps with walnut inks. Alternatively, transfer paints (disperse dyes) could be painted on paper and ironed across. Many companies sell dyed felt in glorious colours, some with toning scrim, fabric or yarns. Look at the 'Suppliers' list, page 57.

Other useful ground fabrics are silk, metallic organza or any suitable soft fabric.

When working on any of these fabrics, a good start is to pull strands from wool, silk or nylon tops, lay them on the background and run the machine over them to mesh the strands into it. Work over them quite heavily and then lift the foot and look at the back of the work where the meshing of the fabrics will result in faint traces of colour. You may like this effect and it is possible to build on it by turning the work over from time to time, working around the faint areas with the same yarn to add pattern and deeper colour. This technique is particularly effective with a felt ground. It is also possible to use the direction of the needling to cause undulations in the surface. Try going around in circles for raised bumps.

Felting needles can also be used to apply fibres to felt but you may need quite a large gauge of needle (smaller number).

An alternative to the soft yarn fibres could be strips of silk, painted or unpainted, lace, net, scrim and so on. They could be worked as a pattern or randomly applied.

A lightweight background fabric which has been textured using the embellisher could be built up into an interesting piece using felt as a base. Enhance the distressed areas with silk tops around the edges. Then cover with a chiffon scarf and work more embellishing on top.

Gold nylon tops, strips of black chiffon and the coiled strips of the selvedge cut from around the edges of a chiffon scarf were covered with a black chiffon scarf and embellished to make a new fabric.

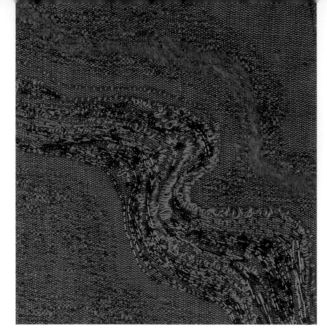

LEFT: Red silk, embellished to make texture following the lines of the machine stitching.

*(Jane Lemon)*

The addition of stitch will complement the embellished surface. It could take the form of lines of free running stitch, outlining a distressed surface. Alternatively, stitched strips could be added to the work, especially silk strips, where the edges could be lost by embellishing them into the background. These options will all be covered as we work through the book.

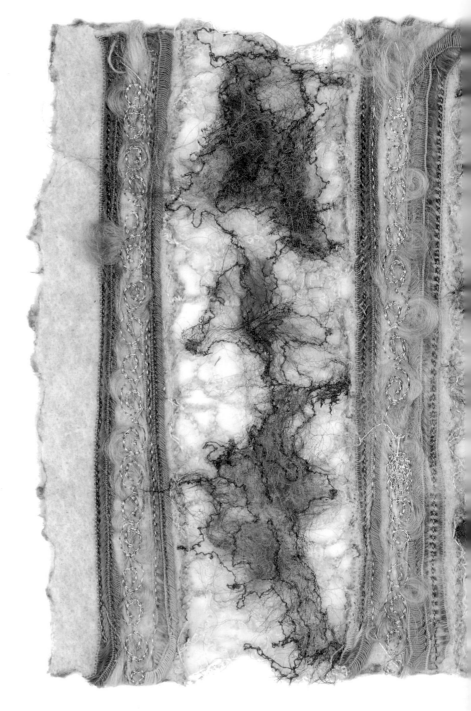

RIGHT: Knitting tapes and yarns embellished onto felt, with teased-out tops and more yarns making a change of texture.

*(Jenny Younger)*

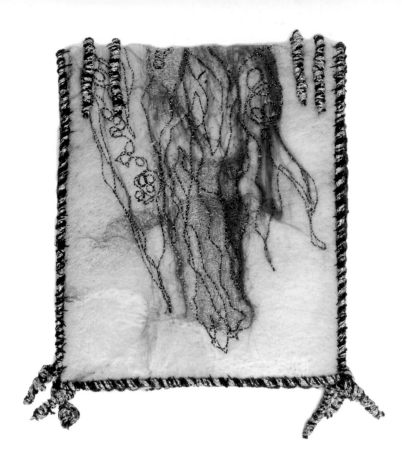

The stitch could take the form of couched braid, wrapped or zigzag cords or heavy metallic threads which could be stitched around the edge of a shape. There are lots of couching stitches that could be worked by hand to add interest. Check out a stitch book to find them.

Don't overlook basic techniques. Shapes cut from a background fabric could have an embellished piece applied from the back. This could be padded, as in the book cover shown here.

ABOVE: Small folded book made from commercial felt embellished with wool, silk tops and a little gold metallic organza. This was overlaid with a chiffon scarf and stitched. Pipe-cleaners were used as both edging and spine decoration.

BELOW: Book cover with padded hearts made from embellished nylon fibres. Stitching adds interest and finish.
(Kit Strathairn)

# applying loose
## fibres and fabrics

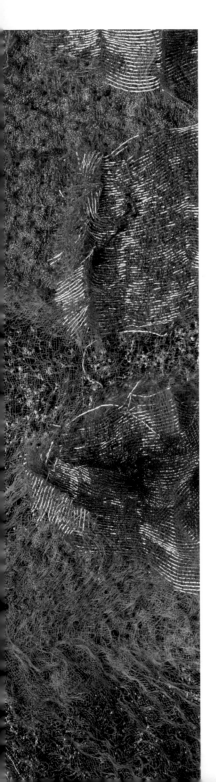

We have already taken a brief look at the use of loose fibres, or tops, and how to apply them to a felted background. Now let's consider some alternative background materials and other fabrics that could be applied. Remember that only soft fabrics are suitable for embellishing. Silks work really well and so do soft scrims. Previously stitched fabrics can be applied and the 'no stiff fabrics' rule can sometimes be broken by using soft chiffon over the top.

Think about possible backgrounds – commercial felt is always useful. The hand tool will be better on a softer felt; old wool jumpers put through a hot wash often make wonderful backgrounds. Don't forget soft velvet, especially the stretchy acrylic variety.

**TIP** If you find that the foot is getting caught up with the loose fibres, lay some coarse net over the top. This can be pulled away after the fibres are attached.

Using any of these backgrounds, consider some of the following.

- Try mixing soft fibres with scraps of silk, lace and scrim. These could be applied to a soft silk background or to painted felt, which looks great with the contrast provided by a lacy fabric.
- The stiff metallic organzas will not apply easily but will become distressed with interesting stray threads. They should embellish enough to fix them to a soft background.
- Think about the design, rather than just placing the pieces at random. Build up with scraps of chiffon to form contrast and give shape.
- Apply stitched shapes to a background, which could be of painted or printed fabric. Soften the shapes by using wool, nylon or silk fibres to integrate them into the base layer.
- Lay down a variety of fabric scraps and novelty yarns. The yarns that resemble tape can be very effective. Use the embellisher to mesh them all together and then stitch a grid over the top. Alternatively, use free machining to outline the shapes.
- Remember to check the back of the work as it will be softened by the action of the embellisher and is often more interesting.

Metallic organza does not mesh well with the background but breaks up into interesting distressed texture. Use a fine fabric over the top to attach more firmly.

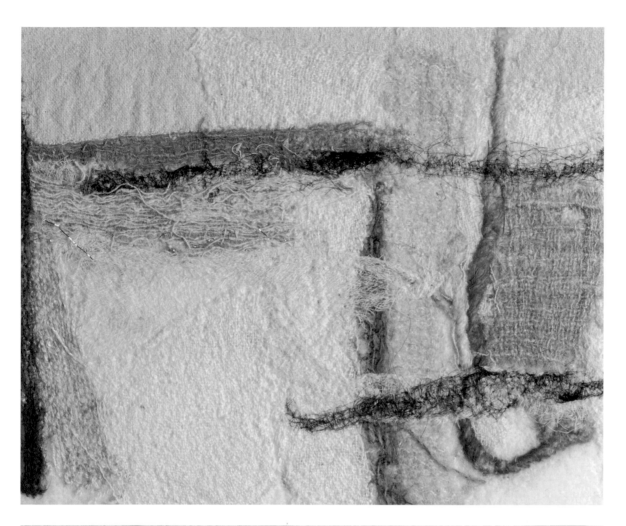

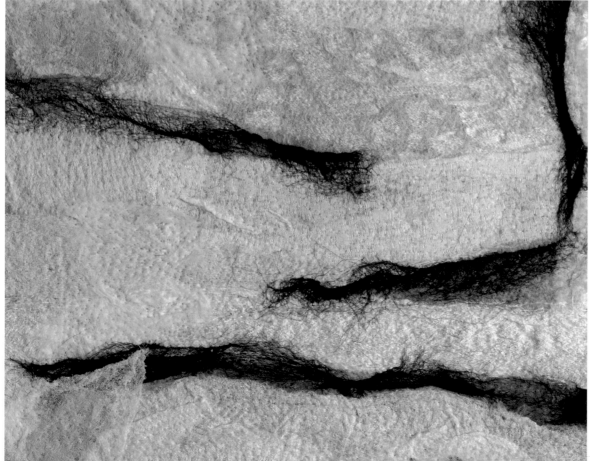

Two small panels with silk
fabrics and scraps of black
chiffon embellished onto felt.
(Amelia Garcia-Leigh)

# applying fibres with the hand tool

Catherine Dormor uses the hand felting process with silk fibres to achieve a wonderful fabric for her work. Catherine says that she was keen to explore the relationship between artist, materials and tools and that it is the tactile elements of the technique that attract her.

She works into a piece of 10 cm (4 inch) foam, laying fabric down first and then a layer of fibre. Using a carved wooden handle with four felting needles, she then needles the fibres into the fabric and foam until they are firmly enmeshed. Once the felting has been completed, then comes the revealing – the point at which the work is lifted off the foam. The process of felting drags the fibres through the fabric and into the foam. The harder the felting and the longer and stronger the staple of the fibres, the more this happens. The 'right' side of the work is the side that is next to the foam.

As the fabric is peeled off the foam, so the luscious surface, which is the essence of Catherine's work, is revealed. Currently she uses Italian silk waste fibres onto silk dupion fabric, which creates a wonderfully rich and lively surface. The random nature of the fibres creates a landscape of felting which varies across the work, creating visual and, most importantly, tactile interest.

Catherine says: 'Working the fibres into the silk gives the appearance of a landscape and the needling becomes a means of drawing with the fibres. This drawing is vital to the finished piece and cannot be hurried. The artworks that result are about the working of that process. I am keen to communicate that the process of making art is as important as the finished piece. We live in a world that is dominated by the visual and yet it is the tactility of textiles that draws those who work with them to that medium. With my work, I seek to create new avenues for an audience to experience the tactile and embodied relationship that exists with my materials and tools as I work.'

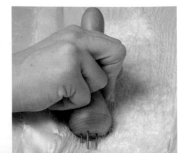

# sheer fabrics

It is often possible to use a soft sheer fabric such as chiffon or organza over the top of a more difficult fabric to apply it. For instance, a painted or printed cotton could be overlaid by chiffon and the chiffon fibres will be the ones that go through to the reverse and become enmeshed. This makes it possible to use a wider variety of fabrics.

Using synthetic fabrics over the top of a layered design offers a lot of possibilities for the heat tool or soldering iron. Try working a chiffon scarf over the top of a piece that has been produced using a layered approach. Then use a heat tool on a heat-proof tray, or similar, to distress it and show some of the surface below. You'll find more on this on page 26.

Try layering up a variety of fabrics with a sheer – such as chiffon or organza – on top. Stitch lines with a sewing machine, about a finger's width apart. Then cut through the top layer and needle along the lines for an interesting faded effect.

ABOVE: Strips of fabrics and knitting tape were embellished onto black felt. A synthetic fabric was laid on top and lightly embellished. After heating, the whole piece was pulled and stretched while still warm.

*(Jenny Belton)*

LEFT: Layers of fabric with a sheer piece on top. Chevrons were stitched and the top fabric was cut between the layers. This cut edge was then embellished.

# pattern making

## using patterned fabrics

Look around the charity shops or car boot sales for chiffon or lightweight silk scarves with rich patterns or colours. Otherwise, paint a white chiffon or silk scarf with silk paints. Simply working this onto commercial felt can bring about a magical effect as the pattern is distorted. This could be enhanced with stitching to add accents or further weight to the patterns formed.

A heavier patterned fabric could be embellished over felt to push traces of the pattern through to the other side. Work with the patterned fabric wrong side uppermost for greater definition. You should find that the traces of the pattern which come through are broken or diffused, giving an effect of faded splendour.

A patterned fabric laid on black felt and embellished from the front and the back. The colours have gone through to the back and the black has come through on the front.

## adding cut shapes

Another way to bring in a pattern element could be to cut shapes from different coloured fabrics, lay them onto a background (velvet would work well) and apply them in the usual way. This would make a good base for stitching.

Shapes could be added in the form of silk carrier rods. These can often be 'peeled' into several layers and this may be necessary before embellishing them. They add a strong pattern element and are good for giving a focal point to an intricate background.

A wide variety of fabrics, cut into small scraps, embellished and then machine stitched in a grid pattern. *(Jenny Belton)*

## bonded appliqué

Ironing fabric to a fusible webbing (Bondaweb) is a good way of making pattern. Try this with a fine silk by painting it, ironing Bondaweb onto the reverse and then cutting out shapes. Peel off the paper and arrange on the chosen background. When the design decisions have been made, peel off the paper and iron onto the background. Then embellish the shapes into the background. If you keep to soft fabrics, this technique will work with the hand felting tool.

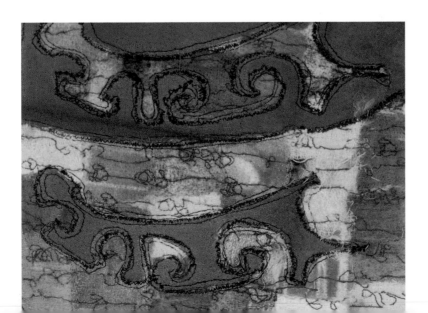

A background of squares was needled onto black felt and stitched. Shapes were cut from fabric ironed onto Bondaweb (fusible webbing) and stitched to apply them to the background. They were then embellished from the back, following the lines of stitching.

## working from the back to form patterns

1 Lay a square of coloured silk – this could be painted with silk paints or be commercially printed – onto some dark felt.
2 Form a grid on the reverse of the fabric by working on the silk, needling in lines, using the embellisher to go over each line several times.
3 Turn the work over and note how the grid has been transferred to the other side of the felt.
4 Now work on the right side by embellishing further, using the grid as a guide. Silk fibres could be applied in the centre of each square or cut-out triangles of fabric could be added.
5 This technique could be extended by 'drawing' into the applied fabric to make shapes, floral effects or abstract patterns.

RIGHT: A square of silk was laid on top of commercial felt and a grid was embellished over the top. The work was then turned over so that the back became the front and geometric shapes were applied.

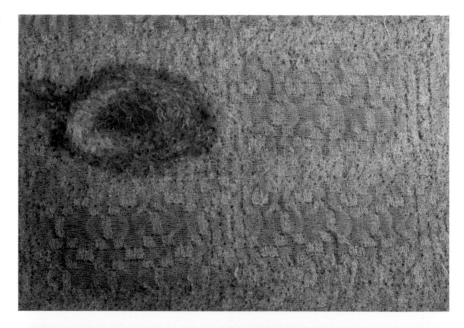

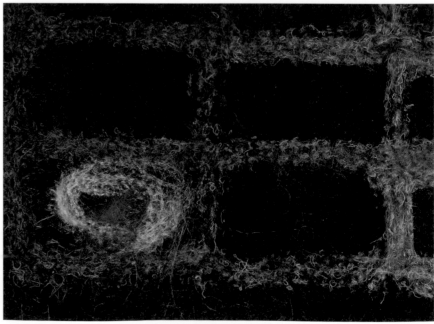

## tissue patterns

It is possible to apply soft tissue paper or Tissutex with the embellisher. Using a fine, soft fabric to hold the paper down will help. Most fine chiffons will work but you could also consider something like painted Sizoflor. This could also give added texture if it is zapped with a heat tool

## computer prints

Using tissue gives the option of pattern-making on the computer. It is possible to use an inkjet printer with this paper in the following manner.

1   Make a design with a strong pattern element.
2   Prepare the paper by applying a glue stick all around the edge of the tissue and sticking it to a piece of ordinary printing paper. It should be well glued down.
3   Feed this through an inkjet printer, setting a margin around the edge.
4   Allow the ink to dry and then cut or peel the tissue away from the paper.

Lay over a suitable fabric and cover with chiffon or Sizoflor before embellishing.

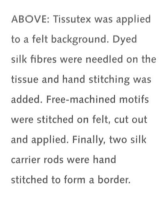

ABOVE: Tissutex was applied to a felt background. Dyed silk fibres were needled on the tissue and hand stitching was added. Free-machined motifs were stitched on felt, cut out and applied. Finally, two silk carrier rods were hand stitched to form a border.

## block prints

No computer? No problem, as stamps or blocks work just as well.

1   Lay the tissue paper on baking paper and colour it carefully. Spray paints are good as the tissue is fragile when wet and a brush can damage it. (It could be quite interesting to apply if damaged.)
2   When dry, use a stamp or wooden block by brushing out some acrylic paint on glass, plastic or baking parchment. Put a pad of kitchen paper under the tissue to be decorated.
3   Place the stamp on the brushed-out paint and make the first impression on blank paper. Then stamp over the coloured tissue.
4   Apply, using the chiffon as before.

Computer prints on paper, laid on black felt and covered with Sizoflor, then embellished.

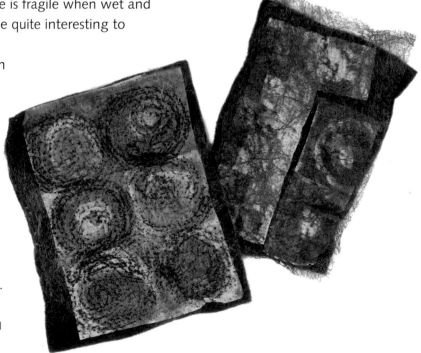

# adding stitch

Stitch can be incorporated into the embellished surface or could form part of the background. Most of these techniques are best worked on the embellisher machine. Here are some ideas.

- Incorporate heavy stitching by working small strips on a soft silk or felt. Leave a border around the stitching – this can be used to apply it by using the embellisher on the unstitched edge.
- Cut a hole in the embellished surface and apply a piece of stitching from the back.
- Use the automatic patterns or embroidery unit on the sewing machine to make patterns, letters or slips. Apply as above.
- Use the sewing machine to stitch on water-soluble film. Dissolve, dry and apply to an embellished surface with further stitching.
- Stitch patterns on a background before embellishing it with loose fibres or fabrics. This stitching could take the form of formal patterns, such as grids or linear forms, or could take an abstract form.

ABOVE: Red chiffon was laid on black felt and embellished. The poppy seed heads were machine stitched in free running and whip stitch. Hot glue-gun trickles were rubbed with copper wax.

(Doreen Woodrow)

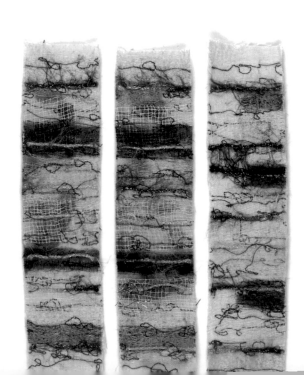

ABOVE and RIGHT: A border pattern using pre-stitched letters and straight stitching on water-soluble fabric was laid on a strip of scrim. The edges were made of embellished and stitched fabrics edged with silky cords.

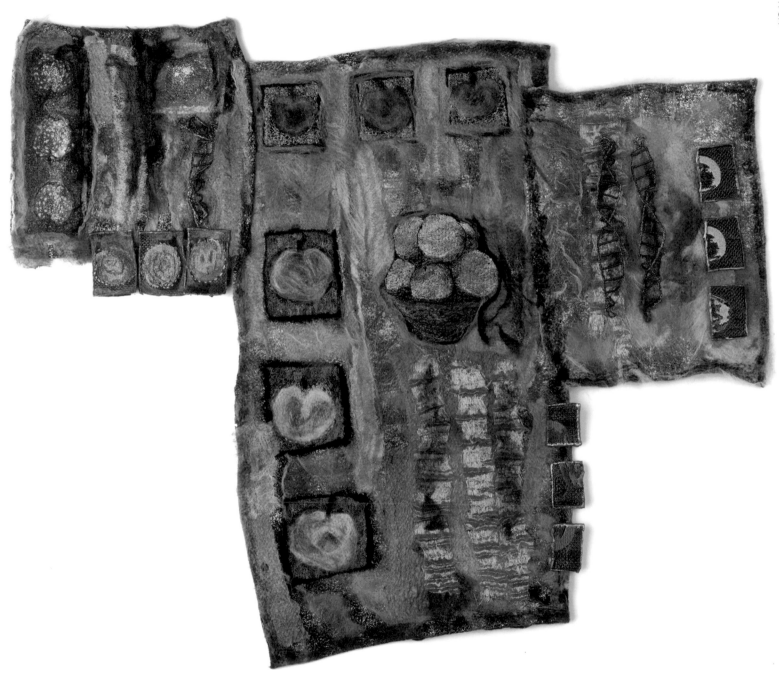

*Genetics of the Fruit Bowl.*

A wall panel based on the keeping of fruit
and the observance of decay. The base is
commercial felt with layers of merino wool
and silk embellished onto it. Metallic organza
was trapped under sheer fabric. In some
areas holes were cut into it and stitching
added. Heavily stitched pieces were also
embellished on top of the background.

# turn on the heat

Synthetic fabrics can often be distorted with heat after embellishing. If acrylic felt is used as a background, that will also distort and create a lacy texture. Do be careful to try out the following ideas in a well-ventilated room, preferably wearing a mask or respirator.

- Trap tiny snippets of thread and fabrics on a background, under a chiffon scarf. Embellish and then use a heat tool on a heat-proof surface to melt some areas of the scarf.
- Embellish torn strips of synthetic organzas and chiffons onto acrylic felt. Heat as described above to distort both fabrics.
- Lace could be embellished onto acrylic felt and then have heat applied by the heat tool. It could be stitched after heating and then the entire surface could be painted. The book cover shown opposite was created using this method.

**TIP** Embellish a mix of natural and synthetic fibres on a background. Some will distort and some will remain untouched by the heat.

BELOW: Before and after. Strips of synthetic organzas were laid on black felt and embellished. The piece was then melted with a heat tool to distort the fabrics.

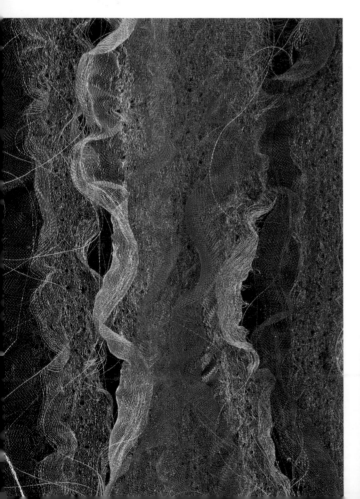 

All the work shown on these two pages has been distorted using a heat tool. The best results arise from the use of a good mix of fabrics.

When considering materials to apply, it is best to work small samples and then try applying heat, as the combinations can be a little unpredictable. Fine chiffon scarves are a good bet when used with the embellisher machine as they allow 'difficult' fabrics to be applied beneath them.

ABOVE: Scraps of lace were placed on white felt and
embellished to secure them. The whole piece was heated using
a heat tool, on the front and then on the back. The book cover
was painted with black writing ink which turned blue on the
synthetic lace but stayed black on the cotton lace. Beads were
dotted over the whole piece, with tiny sequins on the front
edge.

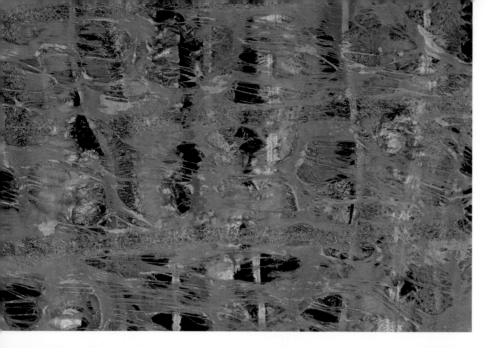

LEFT: A multi-layered piece. Torn strips of painted Bondaweb (fusible webbing) were ironed onto black felt. Novelty yarn was needled over the top. Strips of red organza were needled over this and heated with a heat tool.

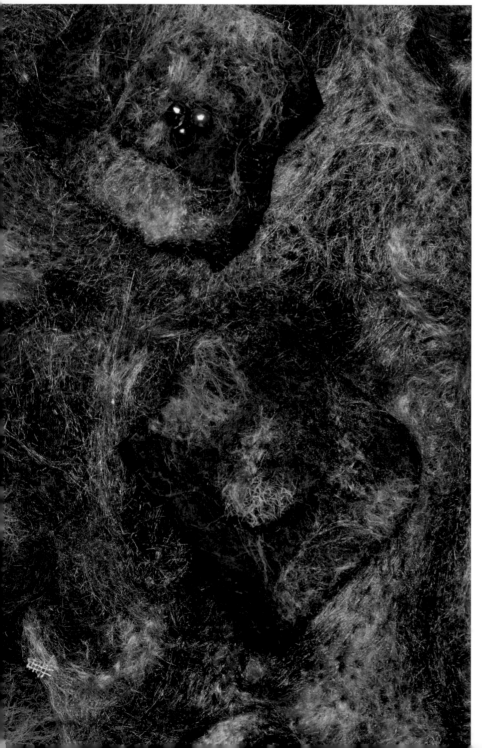

Heat treatments applied to acrylic felt can give interesting puckering and puffed effects. This can be exploited to provide raised areas in a piece of work. Try this technique.

1   On commercial acrylic felt, build up a surface design using silk or merino wool fibres. Keep the design loose and don't apply too much yarn.
2   On a separate piece of felt, apply the same fibres in geometric patterns. Don't make them too small or use complicated shapes. Build up the colours so that the yarns are very slightly thicker than the background.
3   Cut out the shapes, turn them over onto a heat-proof surface and heat the felt on the reverse with a heat tool. You are aiming to shrink the felt rather than melt it away, so don't hold the tool too close to the shape. The motifs will become puffy, which is what you want.
4   Place on the background in a pattern or in a random fashion and apply using free running stitch on your sewing machine.

LEFT: Wool and silk fibres were embellished on felt. Diamond shapes were embellished onto another piece of felt, cut out and then heated on the back with a heat tool. They were then applied to the original background.

# hand tools with heat treatment

The felting needle can also give interesting results when a heat tool is used.

1 Work on an acrylic felt background and apply wool fibres using a single needle tool. Leave some areas open to show the background. It will be more interesting to work in a simple pattern such as chevrons or grids.
2 Couch a line of soft yarn next to the fibres as added interest.
3 Apply a heat tool to distress the felt. This should leave the wool fibres untouched.

Alternatively, try using a sewing machine to stitch cotton lace to an acrylic felt ground. Then needle some silk fibres around the edges of the lace. Leave empty areas of felt and zap these with a heat tool when the work is complete.

1 An acrylic velvet background could have transfoil applied using fusible webbing (Bondaweb). Then needle some wool or silk fibres into this, allowing the glitzy velvet to show in places.
2 Use a single needle to apply very fine chiffon over the top, working it quite heavily in places.
3 When you have applied the fibres, iron fusible webbing (Bondaweb) or very fine interfacing on the back of the work to keep them in place. When complete, zap to dissolve some of the chiffon.

ABOVE AND LEFT: The hand felting tool was used to couch wool fibres and chiffon in a chevron pattern. This was then free machined to add stability before the heat tool was used on the chiffon (below).

# 3 FELTING

The embellisher was designed to produce needle-punched felt, so it's no surprise to discover that it performs very well when used to produce work based on the felting process.

You can produce needle-punched felt from wool tops. Merino wool is a good starting point. It is possible to buy it in wonderful colours, carded and ready to use. The colours can be mixed as you go, making the palette stretch further.

Here's how to make needle-punched felt.

1  Pull a handful from the carded wool tops and lay them flat on the work surface.
2  Pull out another layer and lay at right-angles over the first layer.
3  Pick it up carefully and lay under the needles.
4  Needle all over the surface to mesh the wool together.

Add more layers until you have the depth required.

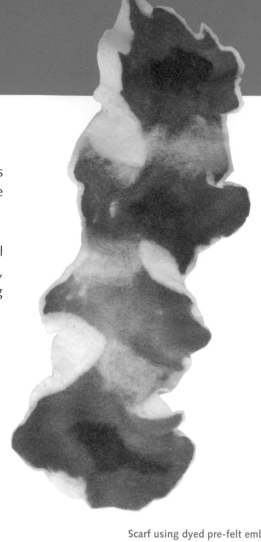

Scarf using dyed pre-felt embellished onto undyed pre-felt.
*(Joy Frampton)*

# using ready-made needle-punched felt

The techniques in this section will work well for both the embellisher and with felting needles. It is possible to buy commercial needle-punched felt and this is very useful. It can be purchased ready-dyed or plain. I prefer the natural fleece as it can be painted, dyed or just coloured by using it as a ground for needling wool, silk or nylon tops. It is especially good as a background for building up pattern or shapes.

The commercial felt is very even and makes a good base for garments, bags etc. where too much texture, in the form of lumps and bumps, may not be what is needed. It is firm enough to take hand stitching and can be gently felted to allow the fibres to be lightly meshed together; this is known as the pre-felted stage. With both the ready-made and the embellisher's needle-punched felt, do try adding some of the novelty yarns available today. There is such a variety – smooth, hairy, glitzy and snippety – and they can all be embellished to the background. They will generally felt very well.

A needle-punched piece using
natural wool and silk fibres.
(Jennifer McFarlane)

Needle-punched felt works well when used as a base for building up designs to be pre-felted, especially when working from a drawn or printed image. Coloured wool can be laid over the base according to the colours in the image. Colours could be mixed as they are laid down. Working like this gives a firm base and saves using too much coloured wool.

# making pre-felts

If you wish to make the needle-punched felt firmer, try the following method.

1   Lay the felt on bubble-wrapped plastic. Put this on a rough surface, such as a bamboo mat and, with net placed over the embellished wool, sprinkle with hot water while rubbing and then use olive oil soap to coat the material.
2   Rub with a circular movement until lightly felted. Rolling up in the mat and agitating will help. It should be slightly firmer than before and will have shrunk a little. I find this pre-felt stage the most useful and often the work can be considered finished at this stage.

More wool tops, silk tops or pieces of fabric can be embellished onto the pre-felt. Alternatively, try hand stitching into the needle-punched felt before going through the felting process. The stitching will not shrink as much as the felt; this produces an interesting result.

To complete the felting process, wet and soap as before, trapping the work between layers of bubble-wrap. This is a very brief description of the felting process. If you are hooked, get hold of Sheila Smith's excellent book *Felt to Stitch*.

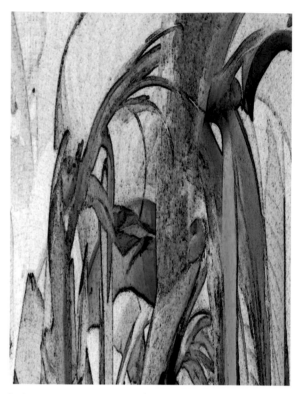

TOP: Computer design using a special effect (Polar Co-ordinates) on a photograph of a Strelitzia.

BOTTOM: Merino wool laid onto a commercial needle-punched background and embellished. The piece was pre-felted and machine embroidered to add emphasis.

Pre-felts make a good base for machine stitching. Heavy free machining in a planned design can form an excellent contrast to the texture of the felt and will encourage an unstitched area of felt to appear lightly quilted. One of our favourite techniques is to use a design to make a pre-felt, as described earlier, and then to use machine embroidery techniques to add depth and to emphasise certain areas.

Pre-felts can also be used for cut-outs to incorporate in standard or inlaid appliqué techniques. In standard appliqué, cut out the shape from one piece of felt and apply to a new background. For inlaid appliqué, two pre-felts in contrasting colours are prepared, identical holes are cut in both and the cut-out pieces from one are fitted into the other before being fully felted to complete the join. This gives two pieces with a counterpoint colour scheme. With the embellisher, it is not necessary to make two pre-felts as holes cut in one can be filled, on the back, with wool tops of the required colour and the machine used to join them. These can then be fully felted or left as they are. What if another fabric such as silk was used to fill the holes? You can see the endless possibilities for these ideas.

**BELOW: 'If winter comes, can spring be far behind?'** *(Shelley).* Dyed and undyed pre-felt with running stitch and seeding to add emphasis to the background and pattern to some of the letters. *(Joy Frampton)*

# deeper into texture

Amazing textures can be made by using natural materials and many of the shops that supply weavers and spinners will have fleece from unusual breeds. Jennifer McFarlane trained as a spinner and weaver and she combines her love of these materials with the opportunities offered by the embellisher. Using a limited colour palette, she combines Ronaldsay, Merino and Gottland fibres with goat's hair, ostrich feathers, wool nepps, noils, muslin and even Angelina fibres to produce work of great originality. Here are some of her ideas:

- Using a fibre such as Ronaldsay or Gottland, overlap and needle the fibres until a soft but firm needle-felt is produced. Then lay a small amount of goat's hair onto the felt and needle carefully across the centre. Don't use too much or you may break a needle.
- An alternative is to lay a little goat's hair right across the felt and needle it in. Add more fleece in places and needle more.
- Mix Angelina fibres with the goat's hair and needle in lines along the surface.
- Make a background felt as before. Then pull out some small pieces of silk noil and form into a circle on the felt. Needle around the circle to apply. Check the back of the work as this can look just as good. Sprinkle some nepps on another part of the felt and needle it in.

**ABOVE:** Silk noil is applied to felt with a circular motion, giving this effect on the back of the felt.

**RIGHT:** Goat hair adds texture especially when pleated.

These rolled felts show what can be achieved by using natural fibres and goat hair.

**ABOVE: A selection of fancy knitting yarns suitable for couching onto fabric.**

There are so many wonderful threads, yarns and knitting tapes available to us now, mainly due to the upsurge of interest in knitting. The embellisher is very good at couching – the technique of attaching the yarns to a background – and many uses can be found for this application.

# what works and what doesn't

Look out for yarns with a texture: thick yarns, thin yarns, hairy or smooth, they can all be used as long as they are reasonably soft. Hand-stitching yarns work well. Look out for odds and ends in wool shop sales as the odd hank, not enough for a garment, will be fine for couching. Some yarns have a laddered effect with thin threads joining them and these do not mesh particularly well; nor do gold braids, closely woven braids or some ribbons. Don't forget that torn strips of soft fabric will couch really well with the embellisher. Combinations work well, as the contrast of smooth and hairy, shiny and matt is good.

The fabric that you are couching on is important and the usual rules apply. Felt, closely woven fabrics, silks etc. are fine but net and open weaves will not hold the couched thread.

**ABOVE: Hairy and smooth yarns couched onto fabric.**

# using yarns

The yarn or fabric will ruche up as it is applied by the embellisher, so cut the strips longer than the fabric, or work down with the ball attached until you are near the bottom. It is not possible to pin down the yarn, so lay it on the background and work slowly over it, holding it loosely in place and adjusting as you go. If the yarn catches in the needles, use net or a soluble fabric on top. In the garment shown opposite, the lines of couched thread accentuate the shape.

*Princess H,* **an Art to Wear piece inspired by the artist Hundertwasser** *(detail below).* **Hand-dyed velvet was twin-needled to provide a contrast to the embellished areas. These were formed from wool fibres on scrim. There is no stitching as all the seams are embellished.**
*(Dale Rollerson)*

Think about the following:

- Couching doesn't have to be in straight, regimented lines. Think of gentle curves, swirls, spirals or grids.
- Even apparently boring yarns can be cut into lengths and knotted. This effect gives a really great texture when embellished.
- Grids are always interesting. Jan Beaney and Jean Littlejohn's book *Grids to Stitch* has some great ideas for sourcing and using grids. Couched threads make ideal grids and are a useful starting point for embroidery.

RIGHT: A book made from fancy yarn couched onto textured silk, previously embellished with silk fibres. A stitched motif was applied and pipe-cleaners stretch over the spine.

LEFT: Velvet with Transfoil and knitting tapes applied in a grid. The vertical tapes have been needled onto each side where they cross, to give the effect shown.

# couching on backgrounds

The background that is used can make a tremendous difference. Just couching lines on a plain fabric could look rather thin and uninteresting. However, a richly worked background would come alive, with the couching adding shape and direction. You can see some ideas for backgrounds on the right (from top to bottom).

- Needle-punched felt was coloured with walnut ink and spray paint. Then knitting ribbons containing a gold thread were embellished onto the felt in soft curves. Finally a layer of black organza was embellished over the top.
- A soft paper table napkin was secured over the top of commercial felt by stitching straight lines with the sewing machine (feed dogs up, ordinary sewing foot). After stitching, the whole piece was dampened with water and a nailbrush used to scrub away some of the paper. Automatic patterns on a sewing machine were stitched on water-soluble film. This was then dissolved to make lacy braids. These were laid onto the background with fine chiffon over the top and couched, using the embellisher machine.
- Plain velvet had Bondaweb fusible webbing ironed onto the surface. The iron temperature was lowered and Transfoil was ironed over the Bondaweb. Painted Lutradur fabric was lightly ironed over the top and zapped with a heat tool. Various yarns were couched onto this, using the embellisher. Some heavier yarns and cords were hand-couched over the top.
- Commercial space-dyed velvet had Bondaweb fusible webbing ironed onto the surface. The iron temperature was lowered and Transfoil was ironed over the Bondaweb. The piece was then zapped with a heat tool. This was used as a base for blue silk fibres and small strips of chiffon, couched in an informal pattern.
- Tea-dyed felt couched with fancy yarns was joined to velvet and further couching was added.

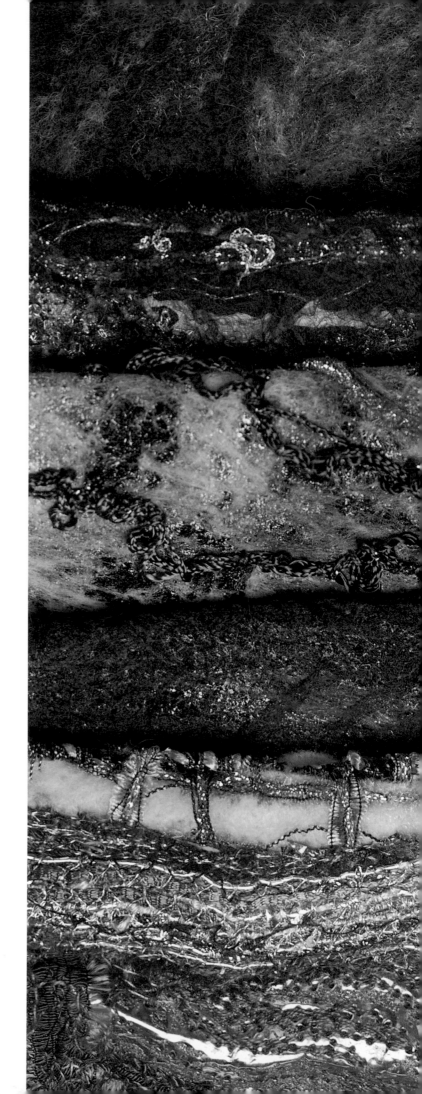

ABOVE: Strips of walnut-inked felt had glitzy yarn couched in lines. These were built up with further strips of felt, stitched with a metallic pattern, and metal shim. A band of couched threads can be seen at the edge.

# combining couching with stitch

Couched yarns can be built up into something really special with the use of stitch, by hand or machine. The felting needles are good for couching; just work on a soft background and use the foam pad underneath. They can also be combined with stitch. Try some of the ideas below.

- Tie knots in strips of fabric or wide ribbons. Couch down by needling between the knots.
- Consider cutting up couched pieces. Felt, embellished with sheer fabrics and couched lines, could be much more interesting cut up and stitched to another piece of work. Alternatively, build up lines of couching and cut into strips to use for ties, belts or straps. This technique can be seen in the piece on the right.
- Machine stitch into the couched lines by hand or machine. Free machining works really well here; imagine lines of couching on one of the backgrounds shown on the previous page. Free running stitches could be used to nibble at the edges of the couching, giving it weight. Working whip stitch, in metallic thread, on the outside of the lines would add glitter and texture.
- Try couching the yarns and work whip stitch in metallic thread as described above. Then lay chiffon on top and stitch again, following the lines of couching. Zap with a heat tool.
- Stitch motifs on soft fabric, cut out and apply with couching to highlight the shapes. Or cut shapes from velvet and needle them to apply onto a felt background. Use a suitable yarn or narrow ribbon to couch around the shapes.
- On commercial felt, use a variety of stamps or objects to print with puff paint. Just using the ends of thick card strips will work well. Puff with a heat tool and paint (just the puff paint) with acrylic paint. Cut into strips and couch onto a prepared background. Add fibres to hide the joins. This fabric is great for bags or book covers.
- Consider layering the material that is couched. For example, you could wrap cord or thick wool in chiffon or fibres to make a chunky roll. Pin in loose swirls to a background and needle each side to attach it. Remove the pins as you approach – don't run over them with the machine.

LEFT: Cut pieces of knitted fabric, knotted short lengths of knitting tape and swirls of a hairy yarn are all couched with the embellisher.

BELOW: Straps made from couched yarns wrapped around notebooks and secured with hat pins. The couching was photocopied and the photocopies pasted on the front of the book.

# couching in pattern

Obviously couched threads can be used to build up pattern and grids can be used here. They could be formal or informal, worked on heavy backgrounds or on sheer fabrics, and the couching could be in the form of yarns or torn strips of fabric.

Here are some ideas.

- A background grid could have motifs applied over the top – this would make a great fabric for a bag or book cover.
- A needle-felted surface could have heavy yarns worked over the top in particular shapes, such as flowers or geometric designs.
- Cut selvedges from chiffon scarves will couch beautifully, often giving a subtle shaded effect.
- Refer back to the idea for needling a soft, silk, patterned scarf onto felt, page 20. Select one with a defined pattern and accentuate this with couched yarns or strips of chiffon.
- A small loom could be used, threaded with fancy yarn. Work a motif in the centre and remove from the loom, taking care to keep the lengths of yarn intact – see photograph on page 49. Lay the weaving on a prepared background and needle around the motif. Then needle along the lines of yarn to couch them down. There are more ideas for weaving in Chapter 5.

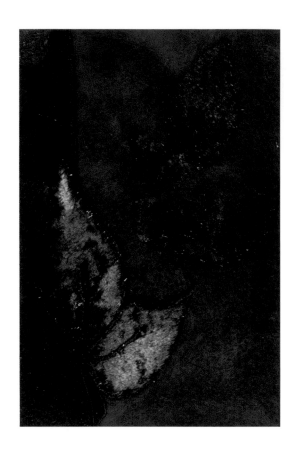

ABOVE: Detail of a bag. Space-dyed velvet was cut into leaf shapes and applied to a background. A darker thread was couched around it to accentuate the shape. More leaves were worked in the same way and merged into the background with silk fibres.

(*Hazel Credland*)

RIGHT: Black chiffon was used to trap silk fibres. It was then embellished to distress the chiffon and mesh in the silks. Finally, yarns were couched over the top in a grid pattern.

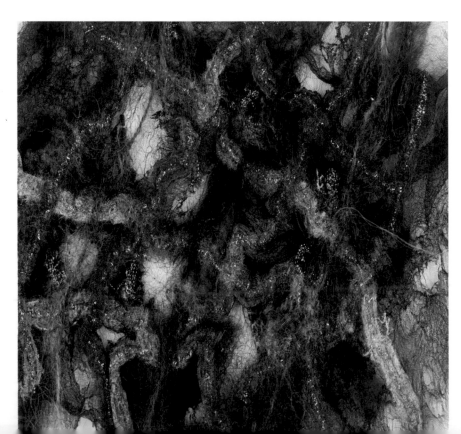

# couching around
# pattern shapes

In Chapter 2 we looked at the use of cut-out shapes which were applied to a background and needled firmly to integrate them with the surface. This merged them in a satisfactory way. However, there are times when it is desirable for a pattern to be more pronounced and this can be achieved by applying the shape firmly to the surface and then emphasising the edges by couching with a toning or contrasting thread. Just work around the edges of the shape.

A further option could be to add more fibres on top of the shape and the couching. You can see this effect in the bag on page 42. A very effective use of this technique is to keep to a simple shape, such as the small squares shown here. In the first photograph cut squares of soft blue, grey and gold silk are applied to felt. In the second image, the piece has been enhanced by the application of couched yarn, strips of sheer fabric and small pieces of stitching on net.

**ABOVE and LEFT:**
Squares of silk were applied to black felt and meshed together. Strips of stitching on net, chiffon scarf edges and fancy yarns were then couched on top. The piece was made into a scroll with beaded, wrapped pipe-cleaners making an edging and small cut pieces of the fabric forming beads.

Just as the embellishing machine can be used to mesh fabrics together, it can also be used to join pieces of fabric or embellished surfaces. Plain fabrics or embellished pieces (needle-punched felt or appliqué, for example) can be folded and needled along the fold to form tucks. Work over this fold several times to make it really secure. Most of the techniques described so far will lend themselves to this method, the only exception being heat-treated or painted surfaces which will be too hard.

# tucks

Fine fabrics, with the tucks close together, will look as though they have been pin-tucked. This is an exciting option with a sheer fabric, such as organza. A heavier material will be better with the tucks further apart. Consider trapping within the tucks. Painted straws or wrapped pipe-cleaners make excellent additions.

The piece of work on the right is on its way to becoming a belt. The basic fabric is commercial felt with wool tops and chiffon needled over it. The construction is simple.

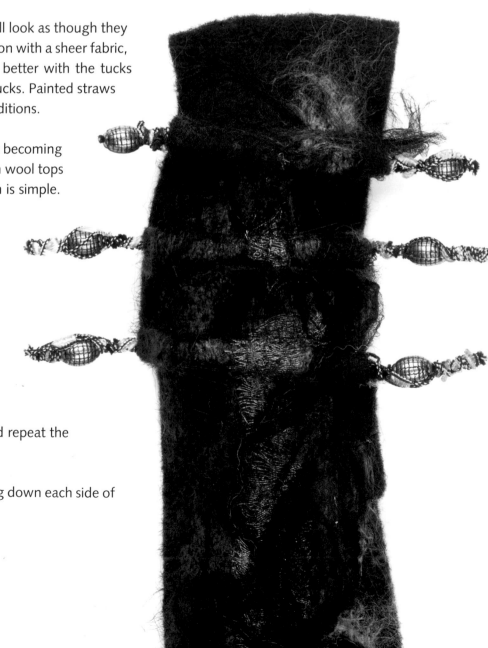

1  Cut a long strip of fabric and embellish by adding fibres. Needle chiffon over the top.
2  Cut the pipe-cleaners to size and wrap them with fancy yarn. A bead could be added at each end prior to wrapping.
3  Lay the wrapped pipe-cleaner on the wrong side of the strip, fold it over and needle several times, catching the pipe-cleaner in the fold.
4  Measure the distance to the next fold and repeat the process.

This technique could be used as strips running down each side of a wall hanging, forming a frame.

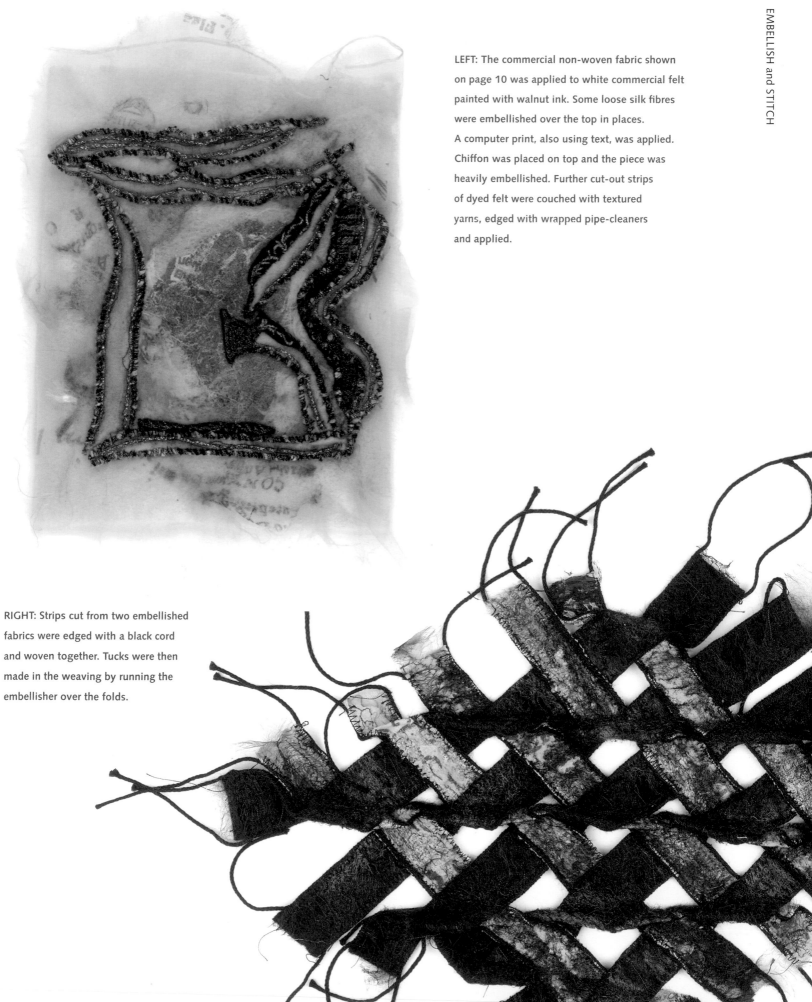

LEFT: The commercial non-woven fabric shown on page 10 was applied to white commercial felt painted with walnut ink. Some loose silk fibres were embellished over the top in places. A computer print, also using text, was applied. Chiffon was placed on top and the piece was heavily embellished. Further cut-out strips of dyed felt were couched with textured yarns, edged with wrapped pipe-cleaners and applied.

RIGHT: Strips cut from two embellished fabrics were edged with a black cord and woven together. Tucks were then made in the weaving by running the embellisher over the folds.

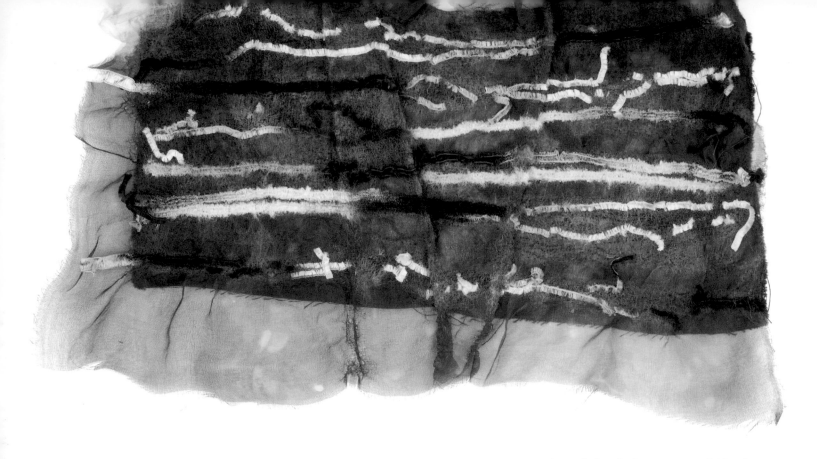

ABOVE: Black-and-white yarns were laid on bronze-embellished fabric and covered with a black chiffon scarf. The result was embellished all over, folded and embellished along the folds to secure them.

# folds

Random folds can be made in the same way as the tucks. They can be formed from an already completed piece of embellishing or stitching or could be part of a carefully designed and planned piece of work. The usual embellishing rules apply – not nets or loose weaves. However, it is possible to use one of the less suitable fabrics, make the embellished folds and then apply the entire piece to a felt background and needle along the lines to secure. Here are some ideas for folds.

- Fold across in a random fashion and needle the folds as you go. If the fabric is not too thick, re-fold in another direction and needle to secure.
- Work folds, leaving a space between them, and then cut out long, thin rectangles or other shapes between the folds. Apply to another fabric and free machine to secure and enhance the cut edges.
- Cut a decorative piece of work – either stitched or embellished – into strips. Lay the strips over each other, either in a random fashion or in a considered grid structure. Pin and then needle over the joins to fasten them together. Then fold and needle to secure the folds.

LEFT: A piece of stitched fabric using dyed muslin scraps was folded and embellished along the folds to make tucks. Holes were cut between the tucks and the edges burnt with a night light. This fabric was placed over another piece of stitched fabric and secured with stitching.

# using a pleater

A pleater, or pleater board, is a very useful piece of equipment and doesn't cost much. It consists of a series of flaps attached to a base. The flaps are very firm and fabric can be pushed into them, from the bottom up, and ironed to set the pleats. The fabric should not be too thick. To use it, work like this.

1 Cut the fabric to the width of the pleater and lay it on top, wrong side facing.
2 Tuck the fabric into the bottom fold with your fingers or a plastic card. Then tuck it into the next fold and continue upwards, tucking the fabric into each fold.
3 Iron well, pressing firmly to secure the pleats. Allow to cool.
4 Gently remove from the pleater and needle to fix the folds. Don't needle all over or you will lose the effect – just in places to prevent the folds falling open.

**TIP** Use a small plastic ruler to push the fabric into the pleater.

ABOVE: A hat, the base of which is made from silk embellished on velvet. Pleated fabric is laid over this and embellished to the base.

(Monica Morgan)

# gathers

As the embellisher needles the fabric, it forms gathers and this effect can be very useful, especially with lightweight fabrics. A material like chiffon, for example, can be manipulated as it gathers and can be persuaded to form a chevron pattern or teased into a marbled effect. This is how it is done.

1   Prepare an embellished fabric, perhaps fibres couched on felt. Lay a chiffon scarf, in a toning or contrasting colour, over the top, so that there is plenty of chiffon overlapping all round.
2   Needle a straight line down the middle.
3   Turn around and work another straight line a little over a centimetre (about half-an-inch) away, travelling in the opposite direction. Encourage the fabric to form pleats which will pull into a chevron.
4   Repeat the stripes, working up and down the fabric – like mowing stripes in the lawn. As you go in the opposite direction, the pleats are pulled to one side, making the chevrons.

Work in a similar manner for the marbling, remembering to start in the middle. Don't work in lines but wander about in a random fashion, pulling the spare chiffon into shapes as you go.

This technique is particularly effective when worked on top of velvet that has had Transfoil and silk fibres applied.

ABOVE:  Walnut-inked white felt was embellished with silk fibres. A pale chiffon scarf was needled in an 'up and down' gathering technique to make chevrons.

RIGHT: A background of dyed velvet was decorated with Transfoil. Some silks were then embellished on top. A black chiffon scarf was needled over this, using the gathering technique to give a marbled look.

# weaving

We touched briefly on weaving in Chapter 4 and there is a lot of potential for working with woven elements and the embellisher machine. It is the fact that strips can be woven and then just needled over the joining points that is exciting. This allows the work to retain its own characteristics with interesting contrasts. Small hand looms or flat wire frames offer further options.

ABOVE: A small loom was used to weave a circular motif. It was cut from the loom and applied to an embellished background, the radiating yarns being couched by needling them individually.

## weaving strips

Collect up a selection of colour co-ordinated strips of embellished or stitched fabric. These could be a mix of solid or transparent fabrics, some could be stitched or embellished, some could be edged with cord or satin stitch and some could be torn. When you've got a little stash, work like this.

- Lay strips of your fabrics on a background, weaving them as you go. Use the embellisher to secure them to the background.
- Work as above but use a chiffon scarf for some of the strips. This works particularly well with dark chiffon as it produces a shadowed effect.
- Make a loose mesh on water-soluble film and dissolve. When dry, weave embellished strips through the mesh. This also works with a coarse fabric with withdrawn threads.
- Work buttonholes in pairs, in a line, on a piece of stitched or embellished fabric. Weave embellished strips though them.

LEFT: Wrapped pipe-cleaners were slotted into a wooden frame. Strips of embellished fabrics were woven through and the ends of the pipe-cleaners were covered with embellished fabric 'beads'.

## weaving with frames and looms

It is possible to buy square or rectangular wire frames; see 'Suppliers' list. Alternatively they can be made from wire coat-hangers with the edges securely bound. Wrap these with fancy yarns or knitting tapes, narrow strips of torn fabric or ribbons. Needle over the yarns to fasten them, being careful not to hit the frame with the needles, and then carefully cut away from the frame. These could be placed on an embellished or stitched background and needled again.

Metal or plastic grids can often be purchased from garden centres in a wide variety of sizes. Many of them are a rather unprepossessing shade of green and need to be painted. A great treatment for them is to use alcohol inks (spirit dyes) in two or three colours. Then weave as before.

Small hand looms can be threaded with novelty yarns and have strips woven between the yarns. Vary the strips and consider weaving narrow strips of metal, perhaps purée tubes, as well as the embellished materials. Most exciting is wrapping narrow pipe-cleaners and wedging them in the slots of the loom. Then weave with a good variety of strips and secure with a pin before removing from the loom. Embellish over the joins, avoiding the pipe-cleaners.

BELOW: A weave worked onto a frame, was embellished on blue woven fabric, then cut away from the frame and embellished again to secure it more firmly.

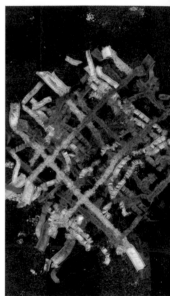

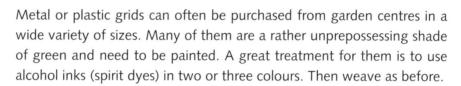

ABOVE: Flat wire frames with yarn wrapped around them can be laid on a background and embellished. The frame can then be cut away.

RIGHT: This book cover was made by painting garden mesh with alcohol inks and weaving previously embellished fabrics through it. The piece was finished with three large fish beads.

# straps

Straps are very useful in their own right. They can be used as fastenings for a variety of items, such as bags, books or jewellery rolls. They can be massed together to form vessels or used in the weaving suggestions given on the previous pages to give extra punch.

Long straps can be made from scraps of fabric or stitching and can be embellished on felt. The embellishing could be simply to hold them in place, blend the edges or give them a texture.

Imagine a long strip with applied fibres and a chiffon scarf forming a marbled surface – similar to the background for the belt on page 3. Now imagine a design free machined on felt with open areas that will be cut out. If the stitching were laid over the embellished strap and free machined around the edges, it would form an interesting and hard-wearing bag strap. The bag could be made from plain fabric with the straps encircling it and forming a shoulder strap.

**TIP** If the strap is going to be used for a practical purpose, it would be a good idea to work some stitching over the top so that it is better able to withstand the wear.

*Let Me Out.* A three dimensional peice, based on mummy wrappings. The detail (above) shows how the straps combine pieces of coloured silk with stitched words embellished on felt and stitched for extra strength. The cover is made of the same silks between two layers of black muslin, embellished on both sides, with stitched words applied afterwards.

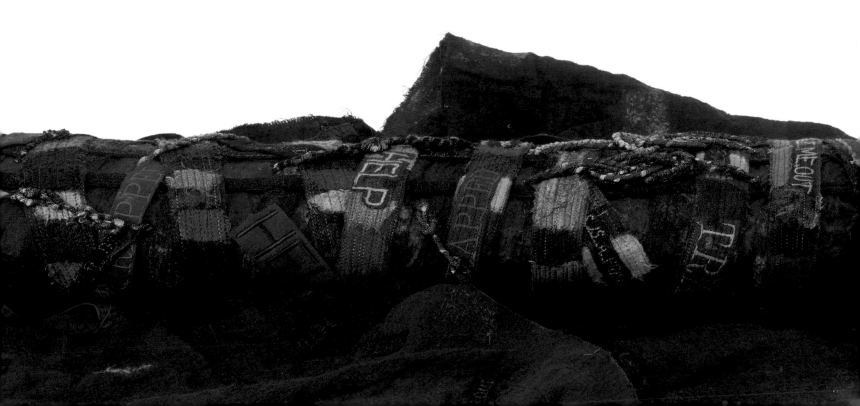

# 6 TAKING IT FURTHER

Although this book concentrates on embellishing techniques to produce a variety of effects and surfaces, the potential of the machine and hand tool for wider applications should not be overlooked. As ever, it is a good plan to work with a theme and explore several elements of that theme before producing paper designs and mock-ups which will help to overcome construction issues.

In the work opposite, the Great Mosque at Cordoba, particularly the arches, inspired a bag. A design board was produced and this prompted further painted and layered papers. These were translated to a needled background of wool felt, coloured with walnut ink and embellished with silk fibres and chiffon. Cut-out arches and machine stitching on felt were overlaid. The arches at the bottom were produced using sewing machine software, as were the straps.

Jan Lovell's work 'Fallen Hanging', was based on agricultural machinery. The designs were painted with acrylic paints and formed a mock-up for the finished embroidery. These were then interpreted in embellished fabrics with added scraps of machined stitched lace on water-soluble fabric. Free running cross-hatching added the final touch.

*Fallen Hanging,* **based on agricultural machinery. The design, to the right in the above photograph is made from paper painted with acrylics. This is interpreted in embellished fabrics.**
*(Jan Lovell)*

A design board based on the Great Mosque at Cordoba.
The bag that resulted from this design source was made by
stitching cut-out felt and stitch shapes, based on Moorish
floral motifs, to an embellished background.

Jean Littlejohn's *Kelim Fragment* (right) was worked on a ground of dyed cotton velvet. This piece contains a series of layers built up gradually and embellished at each stage. Printed cotton chiffon covers the velvet. Further cotton scrim and velvet shapes were bonded and stitched on.

The embellishing process embedded both the fabric and stitching into the ground from the front. It also pushed the blue velvet fibres through to the surface from the reverse.

RIGHT: The two
fabrics used.

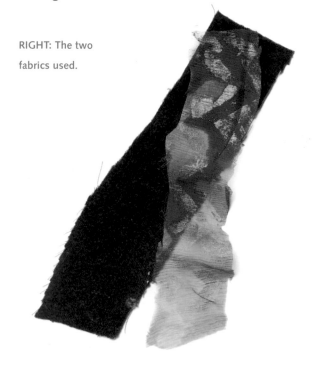

Do use the ideas in the book to build your own textiles. The embellisher machine is one of the most exciting things to happen in the embroidery field, so enjoy using yours and don't be afraid to experiment and have fun.

# glossary

**ACRYLIC FELT**
Felt that will react to a heat tool and give a textured surface. Sometimes called Kunin felt but most synthetic felt works if it has not been heat-proofed. Buy a small piece and try it first.

**ALCOHOL INKS (SPIRIT DYES)**
Paint medium that works on non-porous surfaces. Colours mix well and give an enamelled effect.

**CHIFFON SCARF**
The chiffon (usually acrylic) used for scarves is much finer than that available by the metre.

**EMBELLISHING OR NEEDLING**
The act of running the machine over a surface, or using the hand tool to needle-felt.

**FUSIBLE WEBBING (BONDAWEB)**
A paper-backed webbing-like adhesive which can be ironed onto fabric to join surfaces or act as a base for Transfoil.

**HEAT TOOL**
A tool that gives a blast of very hot air to distress or alter certain fabrics. (A hair dryer doesn't get hot enough.)

**NEEDLE-PUNCHED FELT**
Commercially produced lightweight felt that has not been through the wetting process.

**NYLON, WOOL OR SILK 'TOPS'**
Loose fibres, sometimes called rovings or waste.

**PUFF PAINT**
Paint medium that puffs up with heat. Brand names include Colourcraft and Xpandaprint.

**SLIPS**
Small pieces of stitching that are cut out and applied to another piece of work or fabric.

**TISSUTEX**
A strong tissue-like paper which can be applied using the embellisher.

**TRANSFER PAINTS (DISPERSE DYES)**
Useful for colouring felt. Can be painted on paper and ironed onto synthetic fabrics.

**TRANSFOIL**
A shiny foil with a clear top coat which can be ironed on an adhesive or fusible webbing (Bondaweb). Must be used shiny side up.

**WALNUT INK**
Available as a ready-mixed stain but best value purchased as crystals and mixed with water.